hideaways

hideaways

jane tidbury

photography by peter aprahamian

MQP

This paperback edition published in 2002 by
MQ Publications Limited
12 The Ivories, 6–8 Northampton Street
London N1 2HY

First published in hardback as Huts, Cabins and Hideways in 2001 by MQ Publications Limited

Copyright © MQ Publications Limited 2001
Text © Jane Tidbury 2001
Photography © Peter Aprahamian 2001

Design: Elizabeth Ayer
Editor: Kate John

Additional photographic credits: Mediterranean Summerhouse images on pages 22, 23, 24 and 25 from
Marie Claire Maison magazine, Paris, France, by photographer Marie-Pierre Morel;
property privately owned by Suzanne Slesin and Michael Steinberg.
The Glasshouse images on pages 113, 116 and 117
from Camera Press, London, UK; property privately
owned by Mathias Schründer.

ISBN: 1 84072 448 X

Printed in France by **Partenaires-Livres**®

1 3 5 7 9 0 8 6 4 2

contents

introduction

The idea of escaping from the world we know is a frequent theme of childhood play. But the notion seems to stay with us into adulthood, arguably becoming even stronger as the pressures and pace of the real world make increasing demands on our lives. Perhaps it is a yearning to find a place where we can recapture the innocence of youth, or experience a different kind of existence—one which offers not just a secret hideaway, but a place where one could also live, far away from the adult world, in a private haven. For most of us the dream is to find a place surrounded by nature, isolated and beautiful, where we can find time to connect with the simple things in life, enjoy a slower pace.

The romantic idea of such solitude and adventure is not a modern symptom. For example, in the late eighteenth century, French monarch Marie Antoinette commissioned "Le Hammeau," a model farm, mill and dairy, to be built in the grounds of Versailles. Its purpose was to provide her and her close companions with an escape from their formal lives, where they could simulate the lives of peasants. A century later, fashionable and wealthy families of New York indulged in the rustic timber lodges of the new Great Camps, in the Adirondack Mountains, which drew inspiration from the cabins of pioneering days. And in Germany and Russia, landowners frequented remote hunting lodges for respite.

In the main, the allure of a retreat, both past and present, is that it is temporary. For example, many of us may toy with the idea of living on a desert island, yet how many of us would really wish to be cast away for four-and-a-half years like Scotsman, Alexander Selkirk, the real life character on whom Daniel Defoe is reputed to have based his novel, Robinson Crusoe? Similarly, we are unlikely to pursue our craving for escape to the extremes of writer and environmentalist Archie Belaney, or Grey Owl as he became known—who, in the early 1900's moved from England to Canada to adopt the life of a Native American. However, many of us harbor the same spirit and nagging desire that fuelled Archie in his quest to retreat to far-flung shores.

Such places of escape do not require us to change our lives completely. We do not need to sell up and reinvent ourselves—although some may choose to do so.

What we seek instead is a place that allows us to indulge in our dreams for a while, to find a momentary solitude that fortifies the spirit and rejuvenates our energies. A beach house that looks out onto golden sand and the limitless boundaries of the ocean beyond; a treehouse set high above the ground; a clapboard summerhouse reflected in the still waters of a lake; a log cabin nestled among secluded woodland. Such secret places do not have to be luxurious or modern; rustic charm will do, especially since it is more often the humbler properties that are sought after, and which hark back to simpler times and lifestyle. Indeed, it is by its very nature of being in a backwater, on a lone hill, or at the end of a remote coastal path, that the little country retreat makes more adventurous demands on us. It does not require us to give up on the life we have, merely to enjoy for a while the chance to swap the ordinary for the extraordinary, banish the modern pressures, and claim a little corner of the world for ourselves.

by the sea

T he sea holds a magical allure for most of us. The last bastion on earth over which man still has no hold, it seems unchanged by time or modernity. We may travel upon it, dive beneath it to experience the wonders of sealife, reap its resources, even pollute it. But its spirit remains untamed and unbound; much of its mystery and secrets lie undiscovered since the time of the ancient mariners.

Perhaps for this reason more than any other, we are drawn to the sea as a place of escape. When we stand on a promontory at the threshold of an ocean we can be seduced by the sense of freedom and limitlessness, and feel released from the normal world in which we live. Never still, always changing, it is easy to lose ourselves to every new experience the sea brings.

Coastal landscapes have been shaped in striking contrast to other places we may visit. As the sea retreats, we get a glimpse of that hidden world; soft sand beneath bare feet, clambering over rocks to discover pools harboring shellfish and seaplants. Children's excited chatter caught on the breeze echoes the quintessential family seaside holiday, in which sandcastles and picnics abound. Romantic clifftop views and beachlined shores inspire lovers to steal away for a weekend of sea air, and fresh oysters. Boardwalks entice us to bask in contented apathy upon the smooth, warm slatted surface, our head buried in a good book—or simply to watch the setting sun over the mirrored water.

Coastal dwellings have a unique character. They take on a weathered appearance, bleached by constant exposure to sun, wind, and salt; construction materials are chosen for their durability against these harsh elements. Regular beach houses are built of gray Cedar shingles, or pastel-painted clapboard. Many reflect our relationship with the sea: beach huts that once protected bathers' modesty now provide shady respite for day trippers; fishing huts that are still busy with daily catches now sit alongside those that have been adapted into holiday homes. Even some lighthouses—once manned by caretakers of the light and now replaced by modern technology—have been converted into inns.

Wherever we stay by the sea, it is possible to experience the past in atmospheric comfort. However, the untamed elements are too enthralling to simply sit inside and watch; nature's gift of the ocean tempts us out of doors, to live an open life—to walk a wind-lashed coastline, or to ponder the gentle wash of an incoming tide upon a pebble shore. It is by the sea where we find relaxation and peace.

opposite:
Serene seashore— finding the perfect spot from which to sit and contemplate the view may be the only challenging task of the day.

by the sea

east brother light station

This nineteenth-century lighthouse in the San Francisco bay area now doubles as an unusual inn run by Gary Herdlicka and his wife, Ann Selover.

Set on a tiny rocky island a quarter of a mile out to sea, their home is the stuff of every child's dream: a stunning wooden lightkeeper's house with working light beacon rising up above the roof that offers breathtaking views. Out here life takes on a slower pace, with the promise of untold adventure. There are no phone lines, the mail has to be collected by boat from San Rafael on the mainland, and the water supply consists of rainwater, collected in an underground cistern.

There are four traditionally furnished bedrooms, each with fireplaces and magnificent views through sash windows. The space constraints of the building has resulted in a quirky arrangement with the communal rooms and two bedrooms on the second floor being accessible only by an outside staircase. Meanwhile, in the living room, one can gather round the roaring stove while the wind whistles outside;

opposite:
The journey to the lighthouse begins by launch at Point St. Pablo, and there is a tangible sense of excitement on leaving the real world far behind. Upon their arrival at the island, guests must negotiate a vertical metal ladder to the landing point where their hosts greet them. A long, steep ramp leads up the side of the island—above the rocky surround and crashing waves— to the lighthouse itself, which rests on flat land.

right:
Time and tide go hand in hand at East Brother Light Station.

by the sea

left:
From the small landing, the original staircase winds upwards to a low metal door at the top, leading to the balcony that encircles the light beacon.

opposite and below opposite:
One of about a dozen built in the area, the lighthouse has been guiding ships in the bay since 1873. In the 1970's the station was restored by a non-profit organisation; since then the house has been adapted to accommodate paying guests, the income from which helps pay for its upkeep and preservation.

above:
The interior comprises painted tongue and groove panelled rooms, while lace curtains—woven with lighthouse images—frame the windows. Wooden floors, oil-lamps, and artefacts of seafaring life recreate the maritime atmosphere. The rooms are purposefully uncluttered, reflecting the lighthouse's traditional function while incorporating charming themes of a bygone era.

the dining room next door is set with a large table, where guests gather for sumptuous meals and tales of the sea.

The kitchen seems a gloriously quaint interpretation of the past, filled with the warmth of a large range, well-used pots hanging from a rack, and jars of staple ingredients. The bathrooms also have a simple, fresh style. And as a reminder of just how self-sufficient this existence is, only guests staying two or more nights are allowed the extravagance of using water for a shower or bath!

An automated fog horn emits a gentle, melodic sound from the lighthouse, providing a strangely reassuring constant in the background, as guests retire to bed after dinner.

sea ranch house

This fantastic beach house sits right on the edge of the Pacific Ocean, on a stretch of the rugged northern Californian coastline. Set close to the shoreline, every window in the house is filled with breathtaking seaviews. Despite the presence of other coastal retreats which are hidden from view by a thick enclosure of Cypress trees, one can imagine oneself, the house, and the ocean to be the only things in existence.

The house is part of the Sea Ranch community which spreads out along some ten miles and four thousand acres of forested hills and Pacific coastline, about a two-hour drive north from San Francisco. Once ranchland, development of the area began in the 1960's within a strict framework of planning regulations, which in turn has ensured safe preservation of the spirit and natural contours of the landscape.

Ed and Kathleen Anderson chose Sea Ranch because they love the ocean; the solitude and beauty offer them ultimate respite from the pressures of their work in San Francisco. It was this unique site, enclosed by hedgerow on one side and trees at the rear of it, on which they set their hopes to build a dream holiday home that would guarantee privacy, and seclusion from onlookers, as well as having a wonderful seascape setting.

The Andersons commissioned Californian architects Turnbull, Griffin and Haesloop — already renowned for other projects in the area—to design the house. As a weekend retreat, it had to be large

opposite:
An L-shape layout helps to deflect the biting wind, making passage to the house from the rear more sheltered.

below:
The true pleasure of the house is felt best sitting out on the wooden deck, with its spectacular ocean views.

The side section of the house has three bedrooms and bathrooms, while the master bedroom— with its elegant four-poster bed—is based at the rear of the property, and set on a higher level so that one can still see the ocean. Beams of sunlight emitting from the large windows enhance a sense of warmth and informality within.

right:
The main section of the house comprises a glorious open plan living space with combined kitchen and dining room leading down two steps to the sitting area, itself lined with huge windows that capture the view of the sea beyond. Shaker style has been adopted within: furniture is made of Cherry wood, and the kitchen, with its Ash units, resonates with the building without detracting from its main focus—the seascape.

enough to accommodate friends and their two young children. The design they decided upon for the house was inspired by the local grocery store, with elements of a Nantucket-style fisherman's cottage. The resulting property is less modern than some others in the area: a traditional structure reflecting the look of old coastal dwellings. It includes a lookout tower with surrounding observation balcony, or "Widow's Walk," as it is known in New England, so called because from this vantage point, the woman of the household would anxiously watch out to sea for the safe return of her husband's fishing boat.

The house is built entirely of wood. On the exterior, the silver gray hues of Cedar shingles have already taken on a weathered appearance that helps the building to blend in with the landscape. Inside, the walls are lined with golden tones of vertical Douglas Fir, and overhead, exposed beams enhance the overall simplicity and functional appearance. Entering from the rear of the building through a neat picket fence, one approaches a courtyard with the main block of the house ahead, and a further section running up the right hand side; to the left, one looks out to an expanse of coastline.

A white clapboard houseboat, settled permanently on Hayling Island,
on Hampshire's south coast, England.

mediterranean summerhouse

Imagine waking to the warmth of the early morning sun, streaming in through your bedroom window across an azure blue sea that stretches out to the horizon. This is just one of the delights that first entranced New-York based Suzanne Slesin and Michael Steinberg, owners of this whitewashed stone cottage. Set on the tiny island of Serifos in the Cyclades, a little way from the Greek mainland, the house is built into a rocky hillside and is literally surrounded by views of the sea.

Serifos became virtually deserted in the 1960's when the iron mines were closed down, and most of the occupants at the time had to leave. The huddle of stone cottages, which had once thrived with local people and culture, began to crumble and deteriorate with neglect. But more recently, a few brave souls have rediscovered the place and chosen to make a life for themselves here—albeit in some cases a part-time one—and have begun to restore the properties. Serifos remains a secluded and mostly overlooked holiday destination—unlike some of the more developed neighboring islands—and is quiet, unspoilt, and devoid of any modern holiday trappings.

Already familiar with the Cyclades, the annual escape which Suzanne and Michael make here in the summer could not provide a more idyllic or contrasting break from their normal citybound lifestyle.

Initially, they bought a tiny, two bedroom house on the side of the hill. Then a piece of land behind this came up for sale, rising further up the hillside alongside a rugged path, which leads to a

opposite:
The exterior walls are traditionally finished with a whitewash of lime, the beamed rooms within are enclosed with a ceiling of reeds, and the roof is made of slate.

above:
The magnificent balcony overlooks the calm Mediterranean waters, providing the perfect vantage point from which to enjoy a cooling drink, or in early evening, an aperitif, while admiring the soft illumination of moonlight over the sea.

chapel. They decided to buy the land and expand. With the help of an architect they completely changed the internal space to create a home which now occupies three levels, and incorporates the rocks and shape of the terrain; they have also added an extra bedroom, and additional living space to the original layout. The creation of a grotto-like courtyard which is used for family dining—seemingly carved out of the landscape and overhung with a huge rocky section which provides shelter from the sun—completes the idyllic location.

The interior style reflects the heritage of the cottage but also exudes a personal sense of charm and artistic flair, created from an inspired range of international styles. There are authentic Greek touches: ornate antique mirrors and marble basins bought from Athens; typical furniture and fabrics sourced from the local market, and decorative pottery that blends seamlessly with Moroccan lanterns and American art. The setting has been kept simple and sparse, as befits such a rustic summerhouse.

below:
The main bedroom contains a simple mattress set on a stone platform, with a fresh muslin canopy draped overhead, giving the room a thoroughly romantic air.

In this house the windows are always open, and the sun's energy is always present and inspiring. It is place within which to unwind as well as recharge the batteries, and experience an alternative lifestyle.

mediterranean summerhouse

woodside lodge

A Victorian summerhouse set on the shore of Loch Goil on the west coast of Scotland.

As the owner of a Glasgow-based photographic and film-location-finding company called 1759, it is perhaps not surprising that Iain Hopkins should have secured for himself an idyllic place to live in the heart of the Scottish countryside. But the real gem of his home is a glorious fairy-tale summerhouse painted white with bright red trim.

A few years ago Iain and his wife Kate decided to leave London and, as he puts it, "the 110 miles an hour pace of life," to return to his roots in Glasgow. While viewing a house for themselves and their children, Iain discovered the derelict remains of Woodside Lodge, located at the bottom of the main property's overgrown garden on the banks of the loch.

Completely hidden by huge Rhododendron bushes, the garden had not been touched for some thirty years, and the lodge was on the verge of having to be pulled down. It was built around the turn of the century, and designed with an Arts and Crafts flavor to match that of the main house—a style made popular by Scottish designer Charles Rennie Mackintosh. Despite the huge amount of work required to make it safe and habitable, Iain was in no doubt that its superb location made it worth preserving.

Much of the original structure remains and where repair was impossible Iain used reclaimed materials from other properties, such as pitch Pine for the floor and locally quarried slate tiles for the roof. The structure of the lodge is pretty much as it was originally, however the layout has been adapted to create an open plan, comfortable and easy-to-manage second home. A modern kitchen has been added and the mezzanine level in the eaves has been transformed

opposite:
This picturesque hideaway looks out across the misty waters of Loch Goil.

into a bedroom, and a shower room. The only significant change that Iain has made to the house is the addition of decking around the loch-facing sides. He wanted to create the illusion of being on a boat, and so extended the deck to hang out over the water. The idea works well, and once on board, seemingly surrounded by the loch, it really does feel as though you have cast off from the land.

Inside you are greeted by a color scheme of marshmallow pink. The furnishings are simple and restrained. It is in the details that you find the true spirit and charm of the place—the paddle-shaped spindles of the balustrade that encloses the mezzanine floor; the little wooden ladder (instead of a staircase) that leads up to it; the plate rack that decorates the open partition between kitchen and living space; the large cross carved above the front door; the ornate gables of the roof that shelter the deck below. All these elements, together with an efficient wood-burning stove, complete the lodge's undeniable charm.

above:
The small Celtic cross carved into the red shutters of the bedroom is just one of the charming features within Woodside Lodge.

right:
Natural light coming into the lodge has been maximized using French windows which open onto the open plan living space.

opposite:
A well-stoaked fire heats the ground floor, and loft sleeping area above.

hermione's house

A beach house on the Camber Sands near Rye, in West Sussex, provides a weekend contrast to city living. Owned by Alison and Marcus Riches.

The pastel painted beach house comprises a solid brick base and wooden front, with a simple open plan interior; it is one of five protected beach properties along an expanse of sand dunes. There have been similar buildings here for over a century; the previous incarnation of their own house actually blew away in the great storm of England in the late 1980's. Initially, the new property was only a bungalow with one open plan living area; in 1998 a new roof and second floor were added, providing a gallery in the eaves, while retaining an open plan area for additional living space. The house now offers four sleeping areas. In addition to the new level, Alison put in wood flooring throughout and changed the kitchen to accommodate the new staircase which leads to the gallery.

The beach house interior has a bohemian, eclectic style, with vibrantly colored fabrics and rugs set against simple pieces of furniture, gathered over the years from local second-hand shops. The overall look is one of pared-down simplicity, which helps accentuate the space and light, and makes the place feel welcoming and informal. Pale fabrics in natural fibers help to underscore the seascape's ever-changing palette of colors. Here no one worries about treading sand inside the house, since it seems part and parcel of the beach house's natural setting.

by the sea

right:
At the front the original windows have been replaced with a row of French doors so that the whole of the interior can be opened up to the outside world.

opposite:
More than a bedroom, the gallery above offers a breathtaking outlook across the sea, allowing one to plan the day according to the approaching weather.

Alison and her family are so inspired by the varying moods of the sea, the smells and sounds, that they make it to this weekend retreat every single weekend. Alison enthuses that it is quite simply a therapeutic place to be. In winter they can look out on the drama of stormy seas, while of a summer's evening, they can swim beneath a full moon. A log fence encloses the area around the beach house and prevents daytime walkers from picnicking in their front garden (perhaps the only slight drawback of being right on the beach), but ultimately the house is only fenced in by the sea, the sky, and the encroaching sands.

above:
The wooden deck at the front of the house offers the perfect area in which to sit out, share meals, and be part of the external world.

right:
Providing protection from the raw elements, the many windows create a welcoming sun trap in many parts of the house.

opposite:
Natural light streams in, creating dappled patterns on the wooden surfaces within.

by the sea

in the woods

I n woods we have the chance to truly hide ourselves away among one of nature's inner sanctums. In childhood games, woods offer exciting opportunities for building dens, and climbing trees. Even as adults, this sense of adventure still seems tangible. From the outside woodland can seem impenetrable, and yet basic curiosity urges us to cross the threshold, and peek through the curtain of pine forest. A wonderful sense of exploration comes from walking deep into the heart of a wood, with the canopy of trees shrouding the sunlight, creating kaleidoscopic patterns upon the vaulted ceiling of branches. Then, quite suddenly, the way ahead can open up to reveal a beautiful clearing decked with bluebells, or toadstools, hidden among a lush glade. Footprints are quickly covered by permanent undergrowth, so it can often feel as though ones own tracks are the very first to have trodden there.

By living in the woods, we can revert to nature. We have the opportunity to exist very simply here. Often, shelters become a delightful challenge—without access to modern facilities such as electricity, heating or running water—and the element of basic survival becomes the main focus. Being resourceful becomes the first priority of habitation, perhaps even to learn new skills, such as chopping wood, or collecting water from a stream. The lifestyle takes us away from our everyday world. Even getting to our hideaway can be an adventure in itself, we might have to walk part of the way to get through the trees, or travel on rough, unmade tracks: such a journey creates a physical and mental break from the world we know.

To experience the true joy of a woodland retreat we may perhaps look for more basic dwellings, that blend with the surroundings and offer camouflage, without risk of changing or jarring with the surroundings. An old deserted shed or timber cabin, its roof covered in greenery or moss that has taken hold over time, may be sufficient, with a few essential comforts to make overnight stays possible. To build our own place requires pioneering spirit, especially if it comprises a structure that reflects the buildings of our ancestors and the life they may have lived. By blending rustic exteriors with modern touches inside, the result can be a pleasant harmony of the two. Being in the woods is all about embracing the natural habitat: a running stream, birdsong in the morning, a lone owl hooting at dusk, the rustling of trees, perhaps even the distant sound of an animal's footsteps. And so with our woodland retreat, we experience somewhere remote, secluded, and timeless in its isolation.

opposite:
A lone pumpkin on the step of this woodland den is evidence enough of a much loved and habitable rural hideaway, in New England.

vermont cabin

A primitive, modern structure, inspired by the vernacular farm buildings of Vermont, this woodland cabin provides a back-to-nature experience of living in the wilds. Owned and designed by architect, Ross Anderson.

The limited amenities within the cabin was a conscious as much as a practical decision, Ross' intention being to create a place that was unconnected with the modern world, not just by remote location, but by living a simple existence as well. Here you rise with the sun and rely upon candlelight for illumination after dusk. Having bought the woodland from a friend, Ross was able to realize his dream of having somewhere to go at weekends that would be the antithesis of New York life, and where, as he puts it, there was time to simply watch the snowflakes fall. As a cozy retreat against the elements, the cabin provides the perfect getaway, surrounded by wilderness and inspiring a change in focus upon daily tasks, from chopping wood or working on building projects, to hunting or walking. Ross was also keen for his young daughter to have a real experience of the natural world.

The building draws its origins from the traditional regional architecture: farm buildings such as tobacco barns, corn cribs, and white-painted clapboard houses. These elements are brought together in a modern interpretation, using natural materials that blend with the landscape.

Although only 10 feet wide and 65 feet in length, its clever design has successfully harnessed the compact space to provide every essential in an enchantingly rugged style. The main living space combines kitchen, dining and sleeping areas with a further loft-space bedroom above, set into the eaves: there is a small room for washing, an entrance space or "mud room" (as Ross calls it), and a delightful, semi-enclosed porch.

There is no running water, no electricity, and no bathroom to speak of (just a wash bowl and a mirror), and until recently, taking an early morning constitution required a trip into the surrounding woods with a shovel. A natural spring provides the cabin's water supply via a hand-pump, and also feeds a large pond that Ross made. In addition, he has worked on reclaiming a section of meadowland which provides visual relief from the wilderness.

opposite:
The cabin is remote, set in the heart of a vast woodland region at the end of a labyrinth of winding dirt tracks. From the outside, the cabin appears like a barn in style, with large, sliding doors providing access on either side.

below:
A wash bowl and mirror suffice as the simplest bathroom accessories.

right:
The exterior walls appear to be solid in construction in the form of weathered clapboarding, but in fact, the horizontal slats are spaced apart, allowing sections of light to filter through to the interior. At night, when lit by candles, from the outside, the whole cabin glows like a paper lantern.

left:
Clever design has made use of every inch of interior wall and roof space, with a light, compact kitchen, and a snug sleeping area tucked under the eaves.

below:
The open structure creates a wonderful display of patterned sunlight across the room.

guesthouse hideaway

Framed by trees, this former woodshed in part of a garden in Surrey has been imaginatively transformed by owner, and landscape designer, Anthony Paul and his wife Hannah Peschar, to provide a private woodland escape.

With its moss-covered roof, diamond-leaded windows and soft-blue wood-panelled walls, it has a magical, captivating appeal which promises a cozy and inviting place to retreat. Crossing a narrow rustic bridge over the river, the guesthouse appears, sprinkled with dappled sunlight from the trees. A wooden verandah framed with wild flowers leads up to a wooden front door.

Within, where you might expect to find a quaint, rustic interior crammed with color and objects, the setting is instead beautifully serene and simple, comprising subdued colors and pared-down style. The front door opens into one single room: the house has been effectively designed as one main open plan space to make the most of the available light, and to cunningly suggest the idea that the building is bigger than it actually is. Into the open space Anthony and Hannah have organised a sleeping area, a sitting area, and a kitchen at the rear, with a small shower in a separate room. In the open plan living space, soft sandy-colored walls

opposite:
Had Hansel and Gretel been luckier, they may have stumbled across this unexpected treasure; a sanctuary nestled among lush foliage above a steep riverbank.

below:
The basic structure remains much as it was; the roof and leaded windows have been left untouched, and both aspects possess a charming weathered finish.

and wooden floors add warmth, and blend well with the minimal, Zen-like quality of interior furnishings. The overall effect makes the place feel cozy and welcoming without crowding the room. A waist-high counter partially separates the kitchen from the rest of the room, helping to define the different areas and enclose the space for cooking. Wicker chairs by a window reflect rustic elements, with a wood-burning stove set close by. Every detail has been carefully considered and the beauty of the finished result is further emphasized by its simplicity.

It was Anthony and Hannah's aim, by renovating the house, to emphasize the experience of being in the woods. Indeed, quietly nestled amongst the undergrowth and trees, the guesthouse is something of an idyllic childhood den that by chance one has happened to stumble upon, except this time, it's been designed for grown ups.

below:
A simple bed is arranged against one wall, beneath the windowsill, from which the lush views of trees beyond can be admired.

above:
Large leaded windows are filled with scenic vistas, creating an atmosphere of enclosure and seclusion.

45

tepee

In the wild and wooded surroundings of a mountain retreat in northern New York State, this magnificent tepee provides romantic adventure for day and night-time escape—for adults and children alike. Set away from the main house in a glade, it dominates the view and irresistibly catches the eye.

Tepees were once the typical dwelling of the native North Americans living on the Great Plains such as the Sioux and Blackfoot peoples. Well suited for their nomadic lifestyle, the portable home was sturdy and solid, and provided shelter from the weather. When it was time for the tribe to move on, the tepee would be rolled up and dragged along by a horse. Although this authentic-style tepee replica is more settled in its location, the spirit of freedom and mobility feels inherent in its structure. As with the traditional principles of assembly, a series of wooden poles twisted into a conical frame forms the basic structure—this tepee was constructed using Pine poles. Over this frame, a tough cotton tarpauling provides the exterior covering (originally this would have been made of skins). At the top of the tepee a canvas flap can be opened or closed to allow smoke to escape, and provide ventilation in warmer weather.

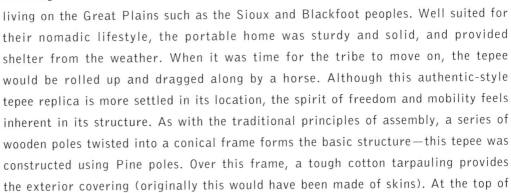

Tall and imposing against the landscape, there is something majestic about the tepee. To enter, you must bend down low to get through the small opening in the canvas, shielded by a flap which can be tied up to allow the sunshine in by day. Once inside, the aroma of grass and woodland mingles with the fire, enclosed by rocks in the center of the interior. The owners have created a rustic interior: huge sections of logs turned on end provide seating; to one side an old wooden bed is thrown with quilts and blankets—in the summer the tepee is used as an additional guestroom to the main house. By day, the tepee has a wonderful quality that reminds one of the excitement of camping as a child and being close to the land. And at night, while gathered around the fire, the atmosphere feels electric, making one feel tucked away in this magical place.

The Cambus O'May station house has been converted into a private retreat. Set on the Deeside line, once run by the Aboyne & Braemar Railway Company, the station was opened in 1876 and saw its last trains run through in 1966. The station house has been beautifully preserved and retains much of its original character.

the doll house

In a secluded inlet of Cape Cod close to the sea a tiny wooden house has been transformed into a cozy private weekend retreat. Owned by Gayle and John Miller.

The Millers' long love affair with Cape Cod stems from the holidays they both spent there in childhood. Once married, they continued to visit the region and brought their own children here every summer; camping on the beach, then over the years graduating from camper van to motor home. In their time they have explored nearly the whole coastline from Bourne at the start, right out to Provincetown some 150 miles further along at its tip.

Their plan had always been to buy a place to which eventually they would settle and retire. It was not until one autumn, a few years ago, with their three children grown up and living away from home that at last their dream—the Doll House—became a reality.

Built in 1948 as a holiday rental home, the property is set close to the town of Sandwich in a small community of homes less than a mile from the sea. Sandwich has remained undeveloped and is very much like the old Cape Cod Gayle used to know as a child and this factor proved a major attraction to the area. In the 1950's, the cottage acquired its rather endearing local status as the Doll House. When the Millers moved in, the whole of the interior was made up of a dark natural wood. In an effort to cheat the dimensions, they added a bright coat of white paint.

right:
Despite its limited size, the property possesses neat proportions and all the essentials have been cleverly accommodated inside: living room, bedroom, bathroom and kitchen.

right:
Finishing touches of Americana style with a nautical theme reflect the Millers' love of water and also conveys an atmosphere of the New England location.

Small though it is, the Doll House couldn't be more perfect. Within only an hour and a half's drive of their main home in Massachusetts, it is within reach on most weekends. In winter time, things get a little more adventurous: the water has to be turned off to avoid freezing, since the pipes are not set underground. This means they must bring in their own supplies, a factor that seems to leave them unfazed. When more members of the family come to stay—the sofa doubles as a spare bed—the shed in the garden serves as a guestroom. And now the Millers' grandchildren are being shown the delights of the place—a third generation who no doubt are about to continue the family tradition.

above:
The cottage is aptly named **The Doll House** as it is indeed tiny. Both outside and within, it exudes a certain childlike charm.

left:
The rooms are fresh and light, and are deliberately sparse on furniture.

french hut

From its spectacular vantage point, set within the foothills of the Cevannes mountains in southern France, this octagonal hut is situated in the grounds of a sixteenth-century farmhouse, and was conceived by potter Sonia Cauvin. Together with the owners, Sonia was inspired by the timeless and spiritual character of an eight-sided dwelling. The recycled timber structure was built in the middle of a setting surrounded by Green Oaks, with two windows, salvaged from an old French barn. Both windows face south-west towards the mountains.

One-eighth of the roof forms a triangular skylight which provides a wonderful view of the evening sky. The inside is simply furnished in a rustic manner: a double bed, covered with a white Indian quilt; two side tables, made from old stones found on the property, each placed on top of a Green Oak base; an art deco North American quilt provides the sole wall decoration. The only other object in the room is an old painted armoire.

The roof has been extended along three of the outer wall sections, and set at a sloping angle, forming a large shaded terrace, complete with a loose gravel surface. Within this enclosed outdoor space, a table has been fashioned from a recycled carriage wheel and ancient kitchen tiles. Both materials were found on the property, which, until eight years ago, was a working farm producing wine, silk, and other regional products. The base of the table comprises an original millstone. The

opposite:
The inspired octagonal frame gently blends in with the natural wooded surroundings. On a practical note, the design also means the hut benefits from shade and sunlight in equal measure throughout the day.

below:
While the hut is sparsely furnished inside, subtle home touches add to the overall rustic flavor, such as this ceramic and bamboo kettle.

slightly tattered but jolly pink chairs were purchased at a flea market in nearby Anduze, and are said to have come from an old café.

The setting is at once tranquil and timeless, and creates a harmonious relationship with the environment. It is also the perfect spot from which to sip cocktails and watch the sun setting behind the mountains.

The open plan room inside has been painted the palest shade of blue, producing a desirably cool and calm effect, even on the hottest of summer days. If truth be told, as forest huts go, this particular dwelling offers more amenities than most: there is running water (cold), electrical lighting, and a working telephone line.

Various climbers and creepers—Jasmine and Clematis— grow against the outer walls, as well as regional plants such as Lavender, Oleander (Lauier Rose), and Thyme. A new, shaded and three-tiered garden, bordered by stones taken from the grounds, has been planted behind the hut. The choice of plants has been deliberate, having in common many pleasing scents. The final feature is an outdoor shower (cold water, again), built against a giant Green Oak which faces the mountains.

tigh romach

Originally built as a laundry on the Belladrum estate, in Inverness, in the Scottish Highlands, the rough house has since been converted into a small self-catering holiday cottage.

Tigh Romach is Gaelic for rough house, an appropriate name referring to the building's unusual and prickly stone exterior. Specifically designed as a laundry in the 1850's, a falling out with the owner of a neighboring property prompted its positioning at the edge of Belladrum, where the two estates met.

The building's survival and current reinvention involves an equally colorful tale. The great-great-grandfather of current owner Joe Gibbs, bought the estate in the late nineteenth century. And it remained in the family until very recently—Joe himself grew up here. But in the 1970's his mother was forced to sell up, and the estate was then divided. Although only in his twenties, Joe vowed to regain the land for himself one day. Rather amazingly, Joe has managed to gather the core of the original estate back together again. He lives at Phoineas with his wife Leonie and their three children—the estate dower house in which he grew up (the original mansion house was demolished after the Second World War).

Renovating Tigh Romach became a feasible way in which to draw an income from the property, as well as a great opportunity for preserving the estate's heritage. The building itself had been in a ruinous state for much of the last century, and renovation and adaptation for modern living was no small project to take on. With the help of architect Lachie Stewart of Anta Design, the structure and interior has been brought back to life with a feel for today's style, as well as respect for the heritage of the past. For the exterior, traditional lime mortar was used for the repointing while the inside was given an authentic backdrop with Clashach sandstone tiles on the floor, which were culled from nearby Hopeman Quarry.

As somewhere to find a breather from normal life, the rough house could hardly be equalled, providing such an unusual and eccentric place in which to rest for a while. But in addition there is also the captivating scenery, a shimmering pond nudging at the house, and a sprinkling of trees to enclose and seclude the setting. And of course, for those wishing to lose themselves in the romance of history, there is the idea of following in the footsteps of those from a bygone era, in hopeful pursuit of a different way of life.

opposite:
With its spectacular setting of lush parkland, and the surrounding tourist attractions in the Highlands—including Loch Ness—Tigh Romach offers somewhere special for people to stay.

left:
The interior has an eclectic look, mixing traditional details with modern simplicity. For example, the dual level living space incorporates a traditional minstrel's gallery, while natural light, streaming in through skylights in the roof, enhances the feeling of height and contemporary elegance throughout.

above:
As a keen reminder of the quirky building, the bathroom is set in the tower on one side of the house, complete with its curved walls.

top left:
A staircase leads upwards to a bedroom on the first floor, which looks down from a railed gallery to the open plan living space below.

left:
The dining room is clad from top to bottom with Pine tongue and groove, and distressed nineteenth-century pieces of country furniture adorn the room; in addition to these elements, more modern pieces have been introduced, including the wrought-iron dining chairs, which create an informal yet stylish effect.

in the clouds

Standing on top of a mountain or hill and looking down upon the earth below, one is not merely rewarded with a fantastic view. The sensation of feeling actually removed from the world that stretches far below brings a new perspective, a new way of seeing things. The atmosphere at certain altitudes is also noticeably different: the air is clearer, fresher, the sun a little stronger, the sky more open and blue. Landscapes are breathtakingly expansive when viewed from a great height: primary rivers appear as meandering trickles, acres of woodland become neat rows of matchsticks, and all aspects of nature are cast in miniature upon the land.

In the same way, places that lead us high above the ground towards the clouds—for example, a treehouse or alpine chalet—provide a different idea of escape, or type of retreat, and allow us to physically remove ourselves from reality. From this vantage point, living among the treetops, we are afforded sights that would never normally be revealed; with a bird's eye view we can pick out dusty hills in the distance, or watch the morning mist fill the valley below.

Finding such places does not necessarily involve ambitiously scaling a mountain. Simple elevation can be achieved with the design of a building: for example, a house jutting out from the side of a hillside, complete with split-level rooms, and an expanse of windows that will capture the panoramic views. The secret lies in creating a sensation of disconnection, giving the impression that the dwelling in question is suspended above the land. A tall structure set upon an ordinary scene at ground level, for example, an old folly or watchtower, will reveal a magical world once you have climbed to its top. Perhaps the ultimate lofty dwelling remains the cabin in the mountains, where the familiar sight of rolling hills or fields is suddenly replaced by an enclosure of snow peaks and dramatic glacial valleys.

It is possible to create our own heady haven. A tall tree makes a perfect home for a shelter or treehouse. The beauty with a homemade den is that it need not be set very high to provide the sensation of living at an imposing level. Even a few meters raised above the ground exacts a complete contrast to the surrounding world, and prompts a real sense of being cut off, isolated, and beyond contact. Through this feeling of removal and separation from the mundane and the everyday, we may choose, for a short time, to trade in the day-to-day routine with a free-spirited sense of adventure.

opposite:
Retreat to a rural outpost, somewhere remote and yet self-contained, such as this stone tower in celtic Ireland, and pay homage to a vast expanse of sky, and views of unrivalled beauty.

the mulholland treehouse

Set high in the branches among a group of Douglas Firs, this lofty cabin hideaway near Bodega Bay, California, is a truly physical escape from the real world far below it.

If they were ever shipwrecked on a desert island you get the feeling that brothers, Jay and Guy Holland, and their father Jack—who designed and helped build this magnificent treehouse—would survive without trouble, indeed, even seize the adventure as a glorious challenge. Conceived in the adventurous spirit of the Swiss Family Robinson, they have constructed a series of breathtaking walkways suspended some fifty feet above the ground, which lie level with the treetop cabin itself. Initially, they considered alternative routes of access: a vertical gondolier-style winch, or a variety of circular staircases wrapped around the trunk. But in order to achieve the sense of being suspended among the trees in solitude, they settled on the most interesting and challenging way to approach the cabin: from a distance. This also makes life easier for Jay's two American Bulldogs who manage to negotiate the vertiginous ascent to the platform above.

The adventure begins from the top of a metal spiral staircase situated in a clearing opposite the treehouse. The only way to the treehouse is to step out onto the ninety-foot-long slatted bridge that appears to float off into the distance. Stealing yourself to traverse it is well worth the effort, as you get to walk among the tree tops. The treehouse is not just a solitary place—a fine collection of warming refreshments and a mini barbecue make it a delightfully sociable retreat after a long afternoon's walk through the surrounding countryside. From this vantage point, one can view the setting sun before returning to the real world below.

left:
The views of the cabin itself, sitting alone among the branches across from you through the trees, are simply beautiful and unique. At the end of the bridge a platform and a shorter bridge leads finally to the deck and cabin, which offers a delightful escape and the chance to gain a different perspective on the world.

left:

Within, the walls are lined with natural linen and set with huge windows which slide open, enabling you to reach out and touch the branches of the tree, smell the rich aroma of Pine needles, and take in the spectacular views. Simply but comfortably furnished, with leather armchairs and a desk, this is the ultimate boys' den.

opposite:

Made of Cedar wood, the treehouse is set on an octagonal platform; the huge tree trunk on which it is built grows up through the middle. One half of the platform forms the shelter (enclosing the tree within it), the other half is a deck with a high balustrade, and the main entrance point.

right:

Living high up among the branches offers the added appeal of space extension to the outer deck; nothing surpasses sitting beneath a canopy of leaves in daytime, or stars by night.

culloden tower

This elegant folly dates back to the eighteenth century and was rescued from dereliction in the early 1980's. Culloden Tower commands a majestic and imposing presence over the parkland where it is set near Richmond in North Yorkshire. Standing on the edge of a steep slope above the river Swale, it resembles a giant chess piece awaiting the Chessmaster's next move. With its octagonal silhouette and ornate rooftop, the now perfect exterior seems an incongruous sight in this modern world; moreover, the architectural style evokes romantic and heroic tales of chivalry.

Built by politician John Yorke in 1746, in the park of his mansion Yorke House, Culloden Tower was designed as a celebration of the final establishment of Hanoverian rule, following the victory of the Duke of Cumberland's army over Prince Charles Edward Stuart at Culloden, near Inverness. But it was not merely a folly or landmark of commemoration. Inside it comprised two comfortable and elegant octagonal rooms—each with its own fireplace—and was used by the Yorke family as a private retreat.

Neglected over the last hundred years, the tower fell more or less into ruin, with little hope of its grand features being seen again.

below:
The tower was originally called Cumberland Temple, in honor of the Duke of Cumberland.

70

**Culloden Tower
commands
magnificent views
across lush parkland.
From the upper
windows and the
original parapet,
guests can conjure
their own "make-
believe" kingdom.**

culloden tower

However, in 1981, the Landmark Trust—an independent preservation charity that rescues and restores architecturally interesting and historic buildings at risk, giving them a future and renewed life by letting them for self-catering holidays—repaired the fabric of the tower. The trust also reinstated the decorative details that had once graced its interior. Luckily, some fragments of the ornate plasterwork still remained; these were used to make molds for the new sections, which included the fireplaces.

The general layout of the building has been kept very much to the original plan with some minor adjustments to make it a more comfortable residence. Passing through a pair of iron gates at the park's entrance, the tower comes into sight upon the hill. Crossing the building's threshold, the stone-flagged entrance hall leads to a spiral stone staircase which winds its way up one side of the building.

The only nods to the modern age are the kitchen and dining area, second bedroom and bathroom, which have been installed in the square base of the tower. Stacked one on each floor are the two original octagonal rooms. For those with a head for heights there is one more level above the main rooms to explore—a parapet at the top of the tower. Enclosed by a balustrade of decorative pinnacles, it offers unrivalled vistas of the surrounding parkland and the town of Richmond beyond.

above:
The tower's rooms are laced with the most extraordinary plasterwork, like icing on a cake.

right:
On the first floor lies the dazzling blue octagonal room. At its heart a roaring fire provides the decorative focus, while huge arched windows offer magnificent views across the park.

opposite:
Ascending further up the staircase you will arrive at the top room, the master bedroom, decked out in bright green with all its wonderful classical details.

napa valley hideaway

Just off the Silverado Trail, this modern structure seems to hang from the rocky hillside jutting out over the expansive landscape of California's famous vineyard region.

If you live in San Francisco but long for wide open spaces accessible at the drop of a hat at weekends, then the Napa Valley could be just the answer. Less than two hours' drive away, with some 29,000 acres of vineyards, the question of finding solitude simply doesn't crop up. This was certainly what the owners of this modern house were looking for when they began the search for a weekend bolt hole: a sense of space and seclusion that was truly off the beaten track. Set high up on a horizontal ledge, the house that they now have seems to hang above the valley it overlooks, with uninterrupted views across vineyards to the Mayacamas mountains beyond. Even more reassuring was the fact

above:
A terrace and long narrow pool below the house draw the eye to the panoramic view. Extending out above the land it seems to be suspended in thin air.

opposite:
Here, modern comforts create an inviting and informal respite, but never intrude upon the natural earthiness that makes the place unique.

that being an agricultural landscape, the area would never be developed, and so their views and the scenery would remain unchanged and unspoilt.

Created by architect Ross Anderson, the building has used the landscape as its starting point, with every aspect of the house cleverly orchestrated to emphasize the setting. Inside there is a sense of being in a box camera with the windows serving as the lens, bringing the spectacular horizon into focus wherever you look. All this has been created from an unusual location: rather than levelling the top of the hill and destroying the natural line of the land—which is frequently done here— the house is built against the hillside, dug into the terrain as though it had slid part way down. From the driveway, at its entrance, below the stepped sections of terraced garden, the house is strikingly silhouetted against the sky. Built mainly of Redwood within concrete corner casings, the style both inside and out is purposefully simple and functional, almost rugged.

Although small, being just 1500 square feet, the interior feels spacious and light. Above an open plan sitting room with spectacular views across the terrace, two bedrooms are set with raised platform sleeping areas that look out of high set windows onto tree tops of Oaks and Firs. The final, third level is a simple space set in the eaves of the structure. A choice of natural, rugged materials and functional design throughout, reinforce the elemental style of the house.

For the owners, the house answers all their dreams: within easy reach for regular visits, it offers them and their friends a great weekend and holiday retreat where they can swim, eat out of doors, relax in the sun, or just soak up the breathtaking location.

above:
One of the bedrooms has a balcony which cements the feeling further of somehow floating in the sky.

left:
On the ground floor an open plan living space is dominated by the large south facing windows.

opposite:
To emphasize the views, the interior styling is simple and pared down. Here the landscape, nature and survival seem to meld as one.

swiss alpine chalet

Were the original occupants of Ammern farm in Switzerland to visit the dwelling today the only thing likely to surprise them is how familiar everything would seem. For although rail transport provides access when the mountain passes are closed in winter, and some of the buildings in the commune now have electricity and running water, the passage of more than three hundred and fifty years seems to have sent barely a ripple of change through here.

One reason for this is probably the fact that since the first buildings were constructed here in 1640, it has always functioned as a farm. The second reason is undoubtedly due to the more recent intervention of Hermann and Rosemarie Wirthner. Twenty years ago they bought Ammern from the previous farmer and owner when he retired and have since been working on the restoration of the buildings, in an effort to recreate the setting as it was three centuries ago. More recently their daughter, Karoline, has taken up the project and by doing so, has continued the theme of their work and vision.

Ammern is set on open pastureland on the side of a hill tucked away from the road. There is a main farmhouse with a variety of barns and outbuildings which include a mill, a weaving room, and a dairy. Some of the barns have been converted into accommodation for visitors, while another has been adapted as a studio and carpentry workshop.

Local people and friends have also helped with the restoration, donating authentic pieces and architectural details that add to the magical, timeless atmosphere you find here.

But the Ammern project is more than just an attempt to recreate the look of the past. Together the family has rekindled the life of the place as it originally was. They make their own cheese in the traditional way, and

opposite:
All the buildings have been restored with historical accuracy using materials salvaged from a derelict farmhouse nearby.

left:
Elements of a more rustic lifestyle adorn the interior; practical basics such as oil lamps and pewter tableware contribute to a nostalgic atmosphere.

run a variety of craft workshops, including weaving and spinning. More modern accommodation has been created in some of the buildings for visitors to stay.

And now that Karoline's parents are less involved in the day to day work of Ammern, they enjoy the farmhouse as a weekend retreat. The farmhouse offers the purest form of restoration; the interior having been set as it would have looked in the seventeenth century. Solid wood furniture, a log fired range and wood burning stoves for heat with oil lamps overhead for illumination at night.

Ammern is not just about farming. People who come to stay here can also enjoy spectacular scenery. Set in a glacier area, it is an idyllic spot for walks and exploration of the landscape. Equally, it offers a chance to retreat back into history and experience a simpler lifestyle.

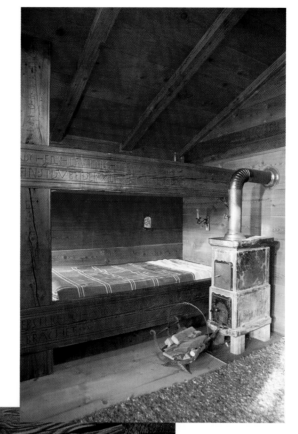

above:
An arrangement of solid timber bunks have been built to fit beneath the eaves. A rustic stove completes the snug atmosphere.

left:
The circular-leaded window panes have the rippled pattern of old, and have been made to the original design.

opposite:
The chalet's interior displays a traditional layout—filled with simple pieces of polished furniture.

treetop office

An old tree provides an unusual setting from which to run a business in this Sussex treehouse.

The brief to John Harris of PearTree (TreeHouse) Ltd, who designed the treehouse was to create a space that would work as an office but also provide room for relaxation. The huge Oak, chosen for the task for its large spanning branches, was perfect for what the owners had in mind. The key design request was that the exterior of the treehouse should reflect the style of the main house—a converted barn—although the building also draws inspiration from the colonial architecture of New England. And where some projects might want simplicity and low-level technology, to work as a busy office all the "mod cons" such as phone line and electricity also had to be installed.

Nestled beneath a canopy of leafy branches, the finished treehouse sits about 10 feet above the ground, reached by a wooden spiral staircase to one side. A solid, cottage like structure, it contains a single open plan room where the owner works, while at the front, a balustraded verandah provides a place for relaxation and entertaining. Constructed entirely of Canadian Red Pine, the horizontal tongue and groove exterior walls are stained black, contrasting with the white painted wooden detailing, and mellowed gray Cedar shingles on the roof.

At first one might wonder whether coming to such a serene place is practical for working, yet the treehouse provides the best of both worlds; physically separated from the daily distractions of modern-day life, it makes it possible to focus and concentrate. And one of the real joys is that it has revealed a marvellous and until now, undiscovered view of the surrounding landscape.

on the water

To sit by a clear lake may be all we need in order to feel relaxed, and at peace. A lakeside setting has to it a quiet, graceful presence that imbues in us a contemplative mood, and a sense of solitude. Historically, man settled beside natural springs or a reliable water source; whole communities have thrived upon the many valuable attributes of this natural resource, which has contributed to the trade, transport and health of its people. In modern times, however, it is more the spiritual quality of water that we pursue, when choosing a lakeside dwelling.

The natural environments that thrive around freshwater areas also provide an organic setting for an abundance of life: a thicket of reeds protruding from the water's edge, rustling in the breeze; the sweeping majesty of a willow tree tracing the ripples in the water with its fine branches; a haze of texture and camouflage along wild and unkempt riverbanks; a haven of dragonflies and waterfowl fleecing the crystal waters for food. Finally, a more mysterious world of plantlife and animals lurk just beneath the water's surface, among the mottled shadows.

Water also absorbs and rebounds the world around it, by reflecting images, and extending the horizons of reality. It plays with the sunlight in myriad patterns, which are at once dispersed by the gentlest breeze, and then made anew. Changing seasons trigger different tones and atmospheres. In rural locations, a place of retreat beside a lake takes on an added dimension, not just to look at but to experience its unique qualities more directly, such as taking a rowing boat out into its center, or going for a swim. Alternatively, we can create a simple setting for a waterside dwelling within the space of our gardens—where a simple pond, stocked with water lilies or reeds, can be the focal setting for a summerhouse or temporary home.

For more dramatic effect, we might choose to spend time by a river where the flowing water brings new sounds and smells as it brushes past the land, and carries life along with it. In summer its pace may slow as if by the power of a sunny, laid-back day; in winter, the flow quickens with more urgency, coursing powerfully along its route.

A deck extending out from a cottage or boathouse over the water is an ideal place from which to soak up the tranquil atmosphere. From here we can feel cast off from the land, free to follow wherever the elements may lead us—the worries of the real world left far behind.

opposite:
Private shrine to nature—a lakeside haven where the seasons are reflected in clear, still waters.

silver tassie

To be able to leave a busy city environment and relax on your own private verandah, with the river a few yards away, is something many of us might dream about at the end of a long working week.

This has been the reality for Gordon and Jane Edington for more than fifteen years, as owners of their own secluded riverside spot along the river Thames, in the south of England. With a passion for messing about in boats, they had been looking for a boathouse with accommodation above to which they could escape at weekends. After a long and fruitless search, they acquired a simple 1930's bungalow overlooking the river. For many years, the Edington family enjoyed their weekend home and its rural surroundings. However, after thinking more creatively about their weekend hideaway, they (rather ambitiously) demolished the bungalow, and in its place built their dream home from scratch. They wanted a structure that would meld with the surroundings and be as beautiful to them personally as in the eyes of passers-by cruising along in river launches.

Silver Tassie was the result—an extraordinarily beautiful structure—large enough to be comfortable and home-like, yet small enough to maintain easily on a part-time basis. The house reveals an eclectic mix of styles, since the architect Max Lyons of Lyons, Sleeman and Hoare, drew inspiration for its design from, among others, the Dachas of Russia. A dacha, by definition, is not simply a cabin; it is the pride of thousands of Russian city dwellers. Traditionally simple in amenities, a

above:
A reverence for the heritage of the river Thames is seen in unique touches: the name of different river vehicles are etched on one window, and upstairs in the eaves above the gallery, the entire list of Thames' locks appear as a "roll call" of some wonderfully colorful names: Mapledurham, Bell Weir, Molesey, with Silver Tassie set at the center.

opposite:
Set on brick piers (high enough to counter flood tide concerns) the house is built entirely from wood, the material traditionally used for houses in the surrounding area. The exterior comprises Russian Redwood, edged with a verandah of hardwood iroko decking; the interior is lined with Douglas Fir, exposed, for the most part in its natural, golden, state.

dacha is a small, cozy, self-contained rural dwelling, providing the means to enjoy a gentler pace from the fast moving city, and to live closer to nature; it represents a weekend family retreat, whether for recreation or for the practical task of tending vegetable gardens. In essence, Silver Tassie embraces the same philosophy.

In addition to this influence, the Edington's riverbank hideaway echoes the wonderful clapboard constructions of Cape Cod, and the simplicity of Shaker style; combining classically simple and elegant details with handmade, precision-crafted furnishings. Finally, a hint of a traditional Kenyan wooden hut—the country in which both Gordon and Jane grew up—is evident in the layout.

To complete the serene waterside setting, a boathouse has also been built, housing a fascinating collection of water transport, notably a 19th century Cedarwood Canadian canoe, a twenty-five feet long electric canoe, and a skiff.

right:
Details like the carved wooden eaves are just one example of the fancy finishing touches that the Edingtons have incorporated. They were especially inspired by the traditional Edwardian structures, still evident along the Thames riverbank.

opposite:
An open plan living area with gallery above looks out through large windows onto the river, while other views span across the nearby water meadows from different parts of the house. A kitchen, four bedrooms and two bathrooms complete the luxurious setting.

A humble hop pickers shed has been turned into a charming country cottage on the water in a small village in East Sussex.

hopbine cottage

The delightful building, set overlooking a tree lined pond in the rural village of Ticehurst, seems so much part of the landscape that one assumes it must always have been this way. Nothing could be further from the truth. Indeed it not only owes its wonderfully romantic character, but also its very existence, to the relatively recent endeavours of its owner, Tony Dobinson. As a child during the Second World War Tony's family was evacuated to Ticehurst from London, and he loved the place so much that he has maintained a connection with the village ever since. A few years ago he bought, and lovingly restored, Hopbine Cottage.

Hop Pickers Yard (as the property was originally known) once comprised two empty shed-like structures, one of brick and the other of wood, which leant precariously to one side and had trees growing up through its interior. Built around the turn of the century, it once provided basic accommodation for the seasonal pickers working on the farms, who would have slept together on the ground floor, and second level on little more than simple straw mattresses. In more recent years, the wooden shed had been a builders' storage place, and the land in front was covered in junk. Tony decided to divide the property, renovating the brick building and selling it to help fund the conversion of the second, wooden structure for himself.

The shed was set on pillars which had crumbled over the years, causing the building to lean. The whole structure had to be carefully winched from the ground, and suspended in the air, while the supporting pillars were strengthened and rebuilt. The walls were then rebuilt using Larch boarding to retain the same external appearance of the shed; the roof, once corrugated iron, was replaced with Welsh slate tiles to match other houses in the village.

opposite:
This quaint, turn-of-the-century clapboard retreat was formerly a workmen's hostel during the hop picking season.

left:
Of the building itself, only the original wooden framework was solid enough to keep, while the rest of the building had to be remade, to remain in keeping with the period style.

right:
**For owner Tony, the
pond was the easiest
part of the project to
complete, and by
planting mature
trees and plants such
as Willows, Laurels
and Ferns around its
edge, the man-made
addition has quickly
adopted a natural,
semi-wild spirit.**

opposite:
**The ground floor
open plan design
comprises a
kitchen/diner and
living space, with
doors leading out
onto a deck. Beams
of Chestnut have
been added to the
internal structure,
helping to emphasize
the cottage-style
character that now
exists here. The doors
are replicas of those
originally installed in
the building.**

The ground floor comprises an open plan living area, while upstairs, three
bedrooms and a bathroom have been squeezed into the space. But the most amazing
transformation of the site is the pond which the house looks out onto. Despite its well
seasoned appearance, it is in fact, all new and created by Tony. A pond builder by
profession, he says he is fascinated by water and its reflective quality, and the
presence of some form of water element was a key part in creating his dream setting.

And with eight children he is never short of family and friends, with whom
to share weekends — indeed, two of his children have set their hearts on being
married here. It is more than just a simple cottage; it is a place that already has a
remarkable history, both for the building, and the family who have preserved it.

gothic arbor

A delightful private bedroom is tucked away inside this whimsical miniature house at the Menagerie, in Northamptonshire.

Some two hundred and fifty years ago, guests of the Menagerie would probably have been anticipating a sumptuous feast. Built in 1750 as a one room folly which served as a dining hall, it had spectacular views across the parkland belonging to Horton House, home of Lord Halifax. Lunch was traditionally served here daily at three. It took its name from the collection of animals kept nearby which according to Horace Walpole and his companion Dr. Cole, included "raccoons that breed there much, a young tiger, a bear and uncommon martins and wart-hogs with navels on their backs."

After years of neglect and dereliction, following the demolition of Horton House in the early part of the twentieth century, and the division of the estate, the folly was converted into a house in 1975 by the previous owner, Gervase Jackson-Stops and his wife. As well as putting the Menagerie building back together, they also reinvented the surrounding gardens with a quirky sense of fun. The Gothic Arbor is one of two such arbors in the garden, the other is Tuscan in style, and was

left:
There is a genuine twist in the arbor's design: a chocolate-box thatched façade on the one hand, and at the other side of the building, a classical style with a regency air.

opposite:
A wooden bridge spanning the water leads you to the tiny house.

above:
Guests imagine themselves more remote than they actually are—by the very lush, semi-wild gardens that encircle the arbor, which also provide a haven for flora and fauna.

opposite:
The enchanting bedroom has a practical purpose as an additional guest room to the converted Menagerie house nearby.

right:
The delicate leaf lampshade by the bedside evokes a romantic link with such fabled characters as woodland fairies.

conceived as a dining room. It is now used as a chapel.

A winding pathway leads you to the edge of a large pond: across the way, a curious thatched roof comes into view. Upon closer inspection the delightful arbor is revealed, set with the most exquisite rustic façade of gnarled Oak boules and tiny gothic windows edged with Hazel. Something even more enchanting awaits discovery inside—a circular bedroom complete with an Oak log bed set against a bedhead of pine cones. A chandelier-style lamp made from twigs and Pine cones hangs overhead.

Stepping through the door on the other side of the room to the outside, quite unexpectedly the landscape changes. Gone is the wild garden, the rustic trimming. Instead, one emerges through a classical façade between stone pillars looking out onto a formal garden pool and fountain, encircled by clipped Hornbeam hedges. A path running off to one side leads to the main house. It is as though one had stepped from one world to another.

The maze-like garden is made up of two circular layouts: the inner, which surrounds the main house and is traditionally formal, and the outer ring, which comprises a wilder, less controlled landscape. The arbors are set at the border where the two styles of landscape meet.

There may no longer be ferocious wild animals to amaze the curious, but today's house guests can look forward to a magical night's stay. And each may choose which side of the arbor to leave by!

riverside studio

Natural elements provide creative inspiration for landscape designer Anthony Paul, in his secluded studio workspace in Surrey.

Anthony's riverside retreat is not only an escape from the day-to day-distractions, a place to go to unwind, it is also the studio in which he works; the surrounding natural elements inspire and energise him, both personally and professionally.

The studio is set on the banks of a secluded river which runs through ten acres of ground. The barn-like exterior blends in with the style both of Anthony's nearby cottage which he shares with his wife Hannah Peschar, and the landscape itself. Environmental concerns have also influenced its construction, and it is built largely from storm-damaged trees and timber gleaned from surrounding woodland. The floor is made from a fallen Beech tree, and the roof from salvaged clay tiles.

Essentially a large open plan space with a small kitchen at its entrance, the beamed studio is filled with light and stunning views. The simple decorative scheme and minimal furnishings provide a soothing and uncluttered backdrop, bringing the outside world into clearer focus; French doors lead out onto wooden deck which overhangs the river. From here, a series of narrow boardwalks—lined with clusters of tall plants—wind their way to the river. All around the building, water lilies hover on the surface of the water, and huge fronds of Gunnera manicata unfurl around the bank, reaching upwards to the deck. Strong, simple shapes made by large groups of single plant species create striking contrasts of texture and color, giving form and shape to the more rambling elements. The atmosphere of the interior, the sights beyond and those experienced at closer hand out on the deck are constantly changing, providing a sub-tropical environment.

As well as a place for work and inspiration, the studio also serves as a practical base for observation: blocks of new plants, recent discoveries or current favorites, grow around the building, and from here their color, seasonal changes, and durability can be recorded. It is also used by Anthony to demonstrate planting schemes to clients visiting the studio.

opposite:
In the twenty years that he has lived here, Anthony has created a semi-wild garden with a hint of control that reflects his work as a designer and conservationist. The surrounding land also includes a sculptor garden and gallery run by his wife, Hannah Peschar.

below:
The connection to water is important to Anthony as the source of life and is a crucial element for his work. This is reflected in some of the studio's design features.

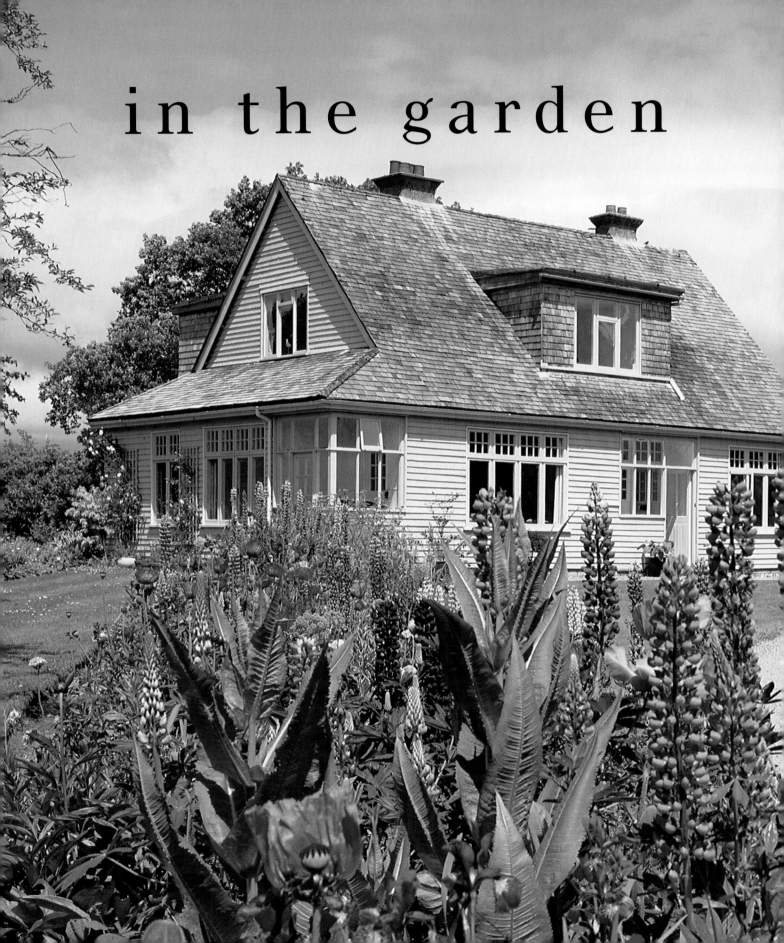

in the garden

Gardens are often overlooked in terms of their creative potential to stimulate personal mood and provide visual drama. An individual garden is often considered simply an extension of our home, a finishing touch or decorative surround that encloses us from the outside world. Clearly, a garden can be more than this. It can be a simple means of creating another world, which, although connected to our daily lives, can seem quite separate and removed from it. A rustic shelter can be incorporated into even the smallest space. Likewise, a unique setting that is both restful and secluded can be the inspiration for accommodating an alternative, part-time dwelling—little more than a quiet corner of nature in which to retreat.

A garden brings the opportunity to experience a sense of familiarity and privacy: we need only share a garden space with those whom we choose to invite. Gardens are also very convenient. There is no need to plan or prepare our getaway—at a moment's notice, at any time of day, we can find a break from routine tasks by simply stepping out of doors. Neither is there need for practicalities, such as cooking, sleeping or a few staple supplies, since most provisions are transportable from home. So our retreat can be tiny—a woven shelter or an arbor of roses. It can also be makeshift: a garden structure such as a greenhouse or a shed can be spruced up for comfort, painted a bright color, or furnished with a favorite chair. A rough floor can be covered with old rugs, and a renovated stove can be installed to keep off the chill during Fall.

A garden enables creative ideas to run free—by offering inspiration to design a unique structure, or to develop a dramatic corner of plants within which to sit and reflect. The scent and color of plants; the degree of light and shade; the landscape's contours and height, and the changing seasons—all are elements which bear careful consideration, when planning a garden to become the main focal point of a dwelling. Moreover, by being close at hand, we can nurture our personal space, and be ambitious and confident with planting schemes or shelters because we will be here to take care of them.

In our own garden we can indulge our fancies, be they dramatic or secret interiors hidden from view, or by simulating an exotic setting or farflung location in our backyard, without having to travel to the actual destination. And like gardens, the dwelling itself can embrace many themes, or be conceived from an eclectic mixture of architectural influences from all over the world.

Tiles fashioned from Cedar shingles make a quaint roof and frame to this summerhouse in Cape Cod, New England.

log cabin summerhouse

In the heart of the English countryside, this Victorian-gothic style summerhouse looks out over a simple garden across a sloping lawn that seems to roll straight off the edge of the world, extending far off into the distance across patchwork farmland. It is a special, private place in which to retreat and to feel totally immersed in the surroundings.

The site on which the romantic folly rests was an obvious spot in the garden since it offered something ornamental from which one could admire the garden and expanse of view beyond. Stepping through a narrow wooden gate in the old brick wall, which encloses the garden and main house, feels akin to uncovering an entrance to a secret world. At first glance, the cabin is not distinguishable through the

opposite:
A swinging bench on the wooden verandah of the summerhouse beckons you to sit a while and soak up the peaceful sounds and scents of the idyllic setting.

right:
The summerhouse's interior provides cool refuge during the warmer months; for all those who venture inside, a veritable feast of quaint furnishings and eclectic art awaits discovery.

surrounding canopy of trees and shrubs; indeed, it seems camoflagued from view. Some way off, draped in a sprinkling of bright green Clematis Montana, the timber frame blends in with the trees that flank it on either side. But then, as shapes and patterns begin to take form from among the wooded curves and colors, the log cabin appears before your eyes, as if by magic.

The cabin was built by Dave Fritchley, a local rustic home and furniture maker with imaginative and resourceful ideas. The exterior, for example, belies a more straightforward approach to construction, the basic building being made of weather board walls with a tin roof, onto which the log finish was added. To raise the structure off the ground, and allow the air to circulate, Dave used six sections of a telegraph pole as supports.

The summerhouse itself is a glorious confection of natural materials: the split Larch logs that clad the exterior reflect the American frontier men's log cabins of the Adirondack mountains; gothic shaped windows and doors finished with decorative patterns in Hazel draw on the Victorian's love of rustic style; sinewy balustrades fashioned from branches of Hornbeam and Chestnut enclose a verandah and soften the exterior. But there is more to the cabin than its atmospheric exterior. It also houses the owner's vibrant collection of everyday handicrafts and artwork. Upon opening the narrow gothic doors in the center of the cabin, an unexpectedly colorful room comes into view.

opposite:
Crotched blankets draped across chairs, amateur paintings on the walls, even doorstops in the form of a couple of knitted tortoises; together, with pieces of china from the 1940's and 1950's, they lend a fascinating charm to the interior.

right:
Bright green walls and a painted floor, inspired by North American patchwork quilts, provide the background to an eccentric display of pieces, and represent a celebration of the creative skill and work of everyday people.

A delightful, traditional Victorian-style summerhouse, complete with verandah, provides a place to relax among the magnificent gardens of the Menagerie in Northamptonshire (see Gothic Arbor, page 97).

the glasshouse

A nineteenth-century greenhouse has been converted into a wonderful weekend retreat at a rural homestead near Hamburg, in Germany.

opposite:
Although only used as a part-time retreat, Mathias has achieved a very permanent settled feel. The small, personal garden around the glasshouse creates a private, cottage atmosphere.

below:
The interior space has been carefully utilized, including the neat kitchen, built into one corner of the interior framework, and hidden from view behind a wicker screen.

Every weekend through the summer months, architect and interior designer Mathias Schründer packs his car and makes the hour and a half drive to his unusual converted greenhouse, set in the gardens of a mansion house. Here, modern comforts mingle with a simpler, quieter way of life in the most spectacular and peaceful setting.

Mathias first discovered the glasshouse eight years ago during a weekend trip to the area. He was looking for a retreat within easy reach of Hamburg when he came across Gut Testorf, an old large farming estate or "gut," still with its workmen's cottages and stables (some of which have also since been converted into homes). He came across the ruined shell of a large greenhouse in what was once the kitchen gardens for the community. It is more than a century old, and had been unused for many years, and most of the original glass panels were broken or missing. But the

in the garden

majestic and imposing decorative iron frame of the greenhouse was still standing, and with it the fragments of the building's original character. Mathias was immediately captivated by the building, and approached the owners of the gut with the idea that he would renovate the ruin himself if they would allow him to rent it from them on a long-term lease. And this is how it all came about.

Although the metal framework was salvageable, the remaining fabric of the building had all but crumbled, and for the most part much of it had to be rebuilt using reclaimed material where possible, to retain the patina and authentic character. Apart from the addition of a few windows in the brick section, the exterior remains much as it would have looked originally. And despite its internal adaptation from plant house to small-scale, part-time home, the layout and division of the interior space too is more or less unaltered. The only real change Mathias has made is to remove a low ceiling in the brick section, to open the space up, and create more height in the room. He has even managed to incorporate modern essentials, such as a kitchen, and bathroom, which is enclosed by partition walls; apart from these, he has left the design of the building untouched.

The house is essentially split into three rooms. The main entrance leads through wooden doors into the brick section where the bedroom is now set. From here you enter the first glass space, comprising the dining area. Ahead, through glass doors one moves to the final area of the house, a glorious, sun-filled sitting room that feels rather like a conservatory. In both the glass rooms the floor has been laid with old bricks set into sand, which create a barn-like atmosphere, evoking both the vernacular origins of the building, and a rustic style.

left:
Dining beneath a
glass ceiling,
whether by daylight
or candlelight, is a
unique quality to this
intriguing dwelling.

opposite:
While electricity and
running water have
been installed, the
property lacks
heating, and Mathias
relies on the glass
panels to absorb any
natural light and
warmth from the
sun. So, for the most
part, the house is
used mainly in
summer.

the glasshouse

More than anything, Mathias enjoys being part of what he calls a special
community, living in a glorious setting surrounded by the grandeur and heritage
of an old country estate. In contrast to Hamburg there is no traffic here, no people
to bother you, only the sounds of nature and a farm at work. For more energetic
days there are walks along the rugged northern coastline which is close by.

A fantastic cavern below ground, exquisitely decorated with shells, creates a mysterious and haunting setting for a fantasy bath house in Northamptonshire.

shell grotto

Standing at the entrance to a grotto, Leonardo da Vinci is reputed to have expressed feelings of both fear and desire: "fear of the threatening dark grotto, desire to see whether there were any marvellous things within it." Standing above the entrance to this shell grotto, set in the gardens of The Menagerie, in Northamptonshire, one sympathizes with his dilemma. A narrow flight of steps appears to lead only into the depths of a deep, dark black hole—a passageway to the underworld perhaps?

left:
Beside the doorway, a figure of Charon, the ferryman of Greek mythology, stands in a small boat.

opposite:
This fantastical play on the mythology of the underworld was designed as a bathing room. Today, to one side of the main space there is a shower room, to the other, a changing area. There is a jacuzzi set in the center of the room from which one can view the decorative creations that surround it.

Descending downwards, daylight disappears behind you, while ahead, a magnificent domed cavern comes into view, set with the most extraordinary figures and tableaux: Orpheus rises from a pool of water playing music to the animals of the underworld. Above him, a canopy of stalactites melting with colors and textures sparkle in the candlelight; elsewhere Cerberus, the three-headed dog that guards the gate to Hades (the underworld), watches over the room. To one who has never witnessed such a sight, it is impressive, made all the more so by the realisation as you get closer that the incredible decorative assembly is formed almost entirely of hundreds of shells, and stones.

above:
The original kitchen fireplace provides atmospheric heating in the grotto, while stars set on the blue painted ceiling glow in the candlelight, and imbue a sense of bathing beneath a twinkling night sky.

opposite:
The elaborate images within the grotto might be drawn from darker stories of mythology, but this simply adds to the mystique and aura of the setting.

The mysterious world of the shell grotto is for the most part a hidden and secret one, tucked away beneath ground—and increasingly one too that has all but disappeared from Europe's gardens. These subterranean caverns are typically encrusted with shells from which figures, animals, floral motifs and patterns seem to grow. Their origins date back to the coastal caves of the ancient Greeks who used these natural formations as places of worship before they built temples. But it was the Italian Renaissance of the sixteenth century that made them fashionable again. In the gardens of France and Italy they became a common sight, styled on the grottoes discovered in Roman ruins which combined paint and shell decoration with water features. Grottoes were not always set underground, indeed when they first appeared in England in the seventeenth century they were often set in a room of the house, in order to protect the expensive minerals and rocks from the climate. In the eighteenth and nineteenth centuries, shell grottoes enjoyed their height of popularity, encouraged by the new enthusiasm for collecting seashells.

This particular shell grotto is a rare contemporary creation. It was completed in 1995 after four years of work, and was designed by the previous owner, Gervase Jackson-Stops, and the artist and sculptor, Christopher Hobbs.

It is set in the eighteenth century shell of an underground kitchen which once served a dining room folly on a large estate. In many ways the grotto pays homage to the history of the place to which it once belonged.

pond house garden

As a designer of open spaces, Jenny Jones is concerned with how people feel and respond within a particular setting. She has created a striking glass shelter surrounded by water, in the heart of her contemporary semi-enclosed garden space, on the Isle of Wight, in the south of England.

Originally little more than an overgrown slope leading down to a ditch and paved area, the three quarter acre garden site offered a completely blank slate, and therefore the opportunity for Jenny to design something unique and highly personal. Her aim was to create a space that would provide contrast and separation from her converted farmhouse, and the hilly farmland that surrounds it: something more intimate and human in scale, a timeless setting where the immediate environment would be the focus of experience.

The garden has been divided into two sections, mirroring the original two levels of the land: a formal, although no less imaginative terrace next to the house, and Jenny's secret raised sanctuary beyond. A narrow boardwalk off to one side leads between two high reflective black walls to the magnificent glasshouse. As you approach it, you realise the walls contain water: a raised pond that encircles the building as though it were partially submerged. The surroundings change dramatically beyond the threshold of this breathtaking building, and a completely new landscape fills your view.

The warmth of the glass cocoon evokes a sense of exotic, arid climes. A series of reflective panels at the boundary form your new horizon, absorbing images of the garden so that it appears to go on forever. An enclosure of sculptural plants and grasses nestles among an expanse of white gravel.

opposite:
The pond house is a peaceful environment in which to sit and read, or simply experience the changing colors of the seasons, and contemplate the patterns in the water caused by gentle ripples.

above:
The glass structure provides protection and shelter from the south-easterly winds that tumble down off the hills.

right:
An ingenious water feature at the front terrace comprises vertical stainless-steel wires from which water—fed from a concealed hose—trickles down onto silver plumb weights, creating a visual delight in the form of a harpstring waterfall.

In many ways the garden has been designed from the inside outwards; the point at which you stand forms the core of the whole layout. To minimize the impact of the pond house as a barrier between you and what lies beyond, glass was the obvious choice, while the lack of structural elements at the corners further blur the perception of inside and out. The use of reflective materials—the water, boundary panels, even the glass of the house—bounce light and images from one area to another so that all these different elements mingle with one another.

By night, the garden is brought to life with a few candles reflecting through the glass, multiplying and lighting up the area, and creating a wonderful setting for entertaining. The glass pond house simultaneously becomes a sanctuary from one world, and a magical gateway to another.

pond house garden

home land

Gary Fabian Miller's Devonshire house sits on the cusp of Dartmoor, at the point where farmland gives way to moorland, and nature's wilderness. From the front doorstep, granite slabs of Hayne Down are visible shapes in the distance, among which sheep quietly graze. Behind the house, a thick wooded valley runs down to a river. Here, the spirit is less about viewing the landscape than feeling part of it.

Home Land, as it is known, was built in 1912 for a retiring vicar on what was once church land. Its wooden clapboard structure—unusual for this area— is lined with windows, filling the interior with mood and colors of the world outside. The evocative presence of nature at Home Land is what first drew Gary and his wife Naomi to the property. It is a

opposite:
Both house and garden are strong reference points for artist Gary; the quality of natural light being a key ingredient for his work.

below:
A vibrant vista of cottage garden blooms: Poppies, Lupins and Grape Hyacinths.

wonderful place where the whole family can spend time relaxing, and an important source of inspiration for Gary's work as an artist, as well as providing him with ideal studio space. In much of his work Gary uses natural materials from the garden, such as leaves and flowers; more recently he has been exploring water as another medium for creating images.

Chic informality sums up the interior style; cool white surfaces meet dark polished floorboards, a combination designed to maximize the impact and beauty of the garden upon the eye: the strident color of a single bloom growing in a flowerbed, the pattern of a leaf on a plant, and the movement of the sun's shadow,

as dappled light streams in from a bold expanse of windows. The fresh rooms evoke a tranquil atmosphere, and a seamless connection exists between them all—a living sanctuary in which nothing is separate, or exclusive.

The enchanting garden surrounds the house on all sides—a rambling, open space which has evolved slowly and intuitively over the years. It is divided into a series of contrasting environments— from formal sections to less controlled wilder areas—and landscaped in such a way so as to provide a variety of experiences. Distributed throughout the garden are plants typical of the area, creating a gentle synergy across the natural boundaries between the house, the cultivated farmland, and the wilder domains.

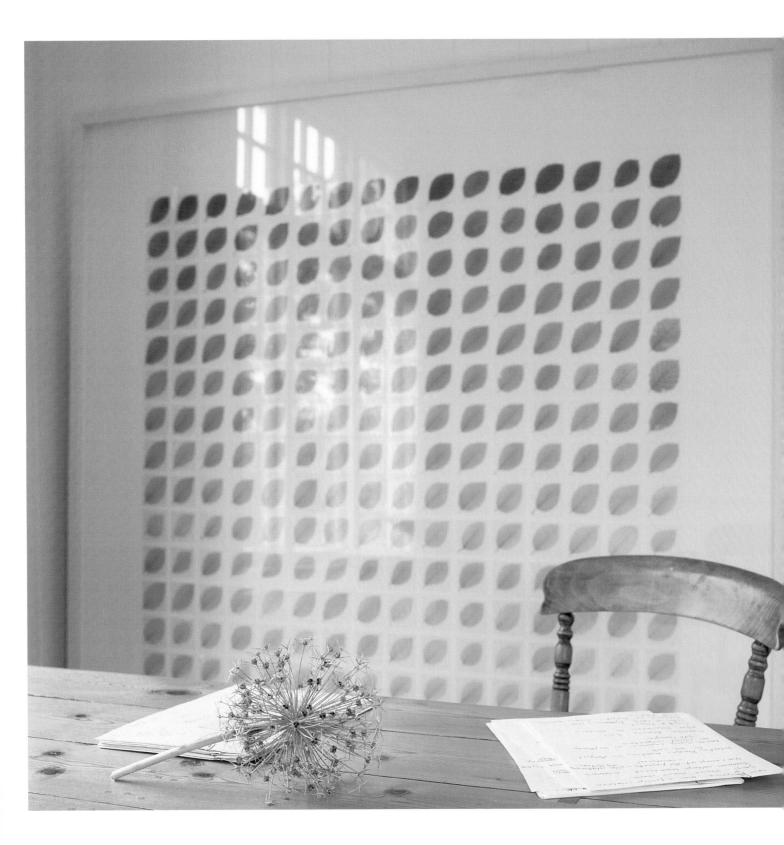

left:
One of Gary Fabian Millier's pictures which he created by shining a beam of light through leaves onto light-sensitive paper. It hangs in the dining room, in quiet homage to nature's seasons.

right:
The interior of the house is painted white throughout to reflect the light, and to present an ideal backdrop against which striking shapes and artefacts in bold textures and colors are artfully displayed.

beyond the fields

S tanding on the edge of an open landscape that stretches out as far as the eye can see, one experiences a palpable lift to the spirits, wherein the mind fills with pleasure from what it sees—often to the exclusion of all else. The immediacy and searing emptiness of the rural scene unravelling to the horizon sparks the imagination, and consumes our thoughts. Undulating fields, Heather-strewn moorland, varigated hedgerows, and shallow brooks provide the props to an otherwise flawless stage.

Perhaps it is the rarity of such experiences that makes their impact all the greater. For the most part, we exist in a cluttered world, filled with cars and people, and are propelled by the stresses of a technological working environment. In a conscious effort to seek relief from these elements, what more incentive than to retreat to a place where the only thing enclosing the view is a great expanse of sky; where one can walk for miles without seeing another person. Equally, it is the chance meeting with local people that contributes an element of discovery and community to many a vast, rural expanse.

Within these little-trodden landscapes one may happen upon a variety of isolated cottages and dwellings. Many of these have a place in rural history—built of local materials, in wood or stone, they are simple and utilitarian—and have survived for many years, having perhaps once been shelter for a farmer's livestock, or a tenant's croft. Restored in keeping with their original character, these dwellings have become well-sought after as country retreats. Flagstone floors, rustic beams, open fireplaces, and leaded windows are just some typical features to be reinstated in these rural idylls.

Equally, the countryside holds a lasting fascination with those who aspire to a nomadic way of living—the open land proving a constant lure for those who wish to live without boundaries. Sleeping beneath the stars, cooking over a campfire, languidly following country roads, or walking rural tracks oblivious to the pressure of time, taking life at a different pace—in many respects this is a greater way to live. However, the desire to be truly mobile requires an entrepreneurial spirit, whether it involves camping in a farflung setting, or moving from one hilltop to the neighboring valley by traditional wagon or caravan. Each mode of transport or mobile shelter lends its own atmosphere of history and adventure to the surrounding scenery—and carries with it a suspense in time.

opposite:
A classical folly is nestled discreetly beyond a field of yellow blooms, in Rousillion, France.

A unique summer retreat on the edge of Bodmin Moor in Cornwall, owned by Tim Hutton, evokes the romance of a nomadic lifestyle, living on the open land, moving from place to place. The idea of such an existence appeals to the imagination and adventurous spirit that exists in many of us. Tim has travelled extensively, and just over four years ago he met an American settler living in the woods in Alaska, in a yurt. This tent-like structure, traditionally the home of the nomadic peoples of Central Asia and still used by thousands today, offered Tim ideas of an alternative way of life. A yurt is gentle on the environment as well as the soul; it barely disturbs the surrounding land, and when packed up, leaves only a few scratches on the soil where it once was.

the yurt

The yurt is deceptively large inside, enhanced by the domed roof which makes it possible to walk inside at full height. This in turn adds to the sense of space and airiness.

Tim built his own yurt which he erected on the woodland he manages with his brother in Cornwall. He lived there full-time for some ten months, establishing his new business venture, Coppice Works, and revelling in the challenge of an alternative lifestyle. Subsequently he has moved to a modern residence from which he now runs the company, organising workshops and making yurts for sale or rent, while using his own yurt as a quiet, private retreat. The best of both worlds.

Tim's yurt is based on those of Central Asia with a rounded domed roof, as opposed to the straight sided roofs of the Mongolian style. Its structure comprises trellis sections for the walls made from Ash, which compact into manageable pieces for transportation. The walls support the domed roof frame made of slender Ash steam-bent poles and canvas; the poles stretch up to the rim of an overhead wheel which forms the center of the roof.

below:
Traditionally, this basic shell would be covered with panels of felted wool, taken from the animals kept by nomadic herdsmen; Tim uses a water-proofed cotton canvas with a colored inner lining, which creates a warm, cozy environment.

the yurt

opposite top:
The peak of the domed roof can be opened to the sky, to allow ventilation for the stove, daylight to stream in, and at night, the chance to gaze upon a blanket of stars.

opposite bottom:
Ropes are used to bind the elements of the structure together.

right:
Unlike a brick built house, there are no dividing rooms or doors to lock, no solid walls to banish the external, raw elements.

The first thing that strikes you about the yurt is its simplicity, the absence of unnecessary clutter or furniture, just the floor laid with patterned rugs, cushions, and decorative textiles, some of which Tim brought back from a recent trip to the Kyrgyz Republic where he experienced the nomadic yurt lifestyle at first hand. At the center, a stove provides warmth, and a focus for the interior around which traditionally the family would gather, cook and eat.

With the smell of grass and trees mingling with the smoke that rises from the stove, and a gentle breeze against the canvas, you cannot help but be constantly aware of nature; either in the fall of the sun and rise of the moon, or the change of the seasons, and the brilliance of a clear summer's day. At the same time, the yurt has a reassuring solidity that feels safe and enclosed, and permanent for as long as you might want it to be.

highland cottage

The bright blue painted exterior of Lochanshelloch Cottage is like a beacon across the landscape. Seen from a distance on the perimeter of wide open cornfields, and tucked away beside a backdrop of pine forests, it is a welcome and reassuring sight after a day's walking.

One of three holiday cottages on the Cawdor Estate in the northeastern Highlands of Scotland, Lochanshelloch Cottage is located in arguably one of the last great wildernesses remaining in Europe: huge skies, panoramic views, dark nights and clean air. The estate comprises fifty square miles of farmland, moorland, and mixed ancient woodland that is spread with a carpet of Bluebells in Spring. Rugged hills, thick with heather in Fall, give way to the untouched coastline of the Moray Firth, and the River Findhorn winds its course down the valley. There is also Cawdor Castle, and the eponymous village close by. Ultimately, all this is about the great outdoors, solitude and nature, and for a few days, holidaymakers can feel like the surroundings are part of their own private garden.

When Colin Cawdor, an architect, moved back to his family home in Scotland to take up the mantle of running and managing the family estate, his wife Isabella Cawdor immediately fell in love with the surroundings. They left London for the Highlands several years ago, inspired to come and live in such a beautiful and remote place. Realising how others would appreciate not just the scenery but also the quiet location, they decided to renovate three cottages on the estate, to provide a contemporary and comfortable base for discerning visitors. They comprise "Achneim," set high on open land looking

opposite:
Set in the remote wilderness of the Scottish Highlands near Inverness, Locahanshelloch Cottage is an evocative hideaway.

141

out over farmland towards the Monadhliath mountains, "Crossroads," which is set closer to the local community and "Lochanshelloch," in its sheltered yet stunning setting.

Originally workmen's cottages, each now offers a traditional, rural retreat full of period charm and character, and provides a welcome contrast from everyday dwellings. Brass beds in quaint sleeping quarters guarantee cozy slumber, and the close proximity of the wild countryside right outside the backdoor makes for authentic,143 simple, and rustic habitation. But each cottage offers its guests modern comforts too, from a well-fitted kitchen to

above:
Wild flowers adorn Achneim's bedroom, while crisp white bedlinen brings a charming freshness so often associated with the Scottish Highlands.

right and far right:
The interior of each cottage combines country living style with light and warmth.

an equally smart bathroom. The best of both worlds is offered: guests can play at living a simple, earthy life without sacrificing any luxuries of home. Indeed, visitors can lose themselves in the serene ambiance, roaming the open land, happy in the knowledge that, just a short distance away, an inviting and cozy house beckons. Once settled within, they can relax and restock their energy levels, in readiness for another day of fun and exploration.

above:
An open hearth in the sitting room and a well-stocked log pile provide guests with a roaring fire, day or night.

romany retreat

For short spells of the year this mid-nineteenth century traveller's wagon or vardo (as it was called by Romany people) is Joe Berens' home. A traditional hurdle and rustic furniture maker by trade, Joe finds traveling the country roads a great antidote to modern-day life; its languid pace of travel offers the chance to experience the countryside more closely. People he meets along the way have more time to talk, and are momentarily caught up in the alluring romance of his way of life.

This is a bow top wagon, identified by its hooped frame of steam-bent Ash enclosed with a green waterproof canvas which helps the vehicle blend in with the landscape. The decorative paintwork on the exterior and wheels is also typical: no two vardos were alike, each carrying the signature of their maker in these colorful painted details.

The interior of the wagon exudes the romance of a largely bygone existence. The small space is fitted with a raised bed at one end while small cupboards line the sides. Overhead, the wooden structure is insulated with carpet panels. At the rear of the wagon a small wooden cupboard or pan-box, set low beneath the floor boards, is ideal for storing provisions, which are shaded from the sun.

opposite:
The decorative exterior and open doorway is typical of the bow top wagon—there is no need for a door since the wagon can be set with its back facing the wind, protecting the interior. The traditional kettle iron, used for cooking, hangs from a crook-shaped rod over the fire. A bench of Hazel and Oak, handmade by Joe, blends in with the natural surroundings.

below:
Set across the end of the wagon's interior is a fitted raised bed, tucked beneath the curved framework.

clapboard farmhouse

The faded grandeur of a nineteenth-century farmhouse near the Catskills mountains in New York State has been reinvented as a quirky family home by designer Barbara Davis.

When Barbara first bought her clapboard house she shared it initially with a family of raccoons and snakes that were living beneath the floorboards. Today, the animal contingent is no less eccentric—her three sheep share the kitchen when its cold, and an untallied number of stray and family cats are equally attached to the place. Based in northern New York State—the area is known as the Boonies, an American term meant fondly which translates to mean "the back of beyond," or "the middle of nowhere"—the farmhouse is truly remote, set on a long empty road shared only with a handful of houses. This, together with its spacious and understated rooms, makes it an ideal escape for Barbara and her four children.

The farmhouse had not been lived in for some fifty years; such untouched places are hard to find, generally because they either fall prey to unsympathetic modernisation or are left to deteriorate beyond repair. But in the case of this

opposite:
Lathe and plaster walls, which are slightly crumbling and laced with cracks, add to the property's faded charm, and rural atmosphere.

right:
Barbara's house provides a welcome journey back in time to a life that was about using the natural elements around us, making do, being creative, and enjoying the simple things—a philosophy Barbara extolls in her work as a designer.

left:
Handmade, textured stencils have been worked across the bedroom walls, and the bed covering has been hand-dyed by Barbara.

opposite:
Bright gingham fabric and hand-dyed cushions, designed by Barbara, bring a splash of color to the interior's more natural hues.

below:
Traditional banisters lead upwards from the hallway to a series of bedrooms.

clapboard house, the roof and structure were at least sound. The oldest part of the house was built at the end of the eighteenth century, a barn with accommodation above. In the nineteenth century, new sections were added to create a small farmhouse. There was an element of modernisation in the 1940's. The original kitchen of that time is still in place, and has been freshened up. Barbara has toyed with the idea of rearranging some of the layout but says she would feel guilty about destroying the integrity of the place. Her approach has been to make good the original structure without tampering with the overall period or classical charm of the house.

Life here can be hard: for example, there is no main line water, the supply is pumped from a nearby well. But arguably that is all part of the fun. And as well as providing open space and opportunities for adventure—the Adirondack mountains are only an hour's drive away—Barbara claims the atmosphere and way of life has made her more creative. Indeed, as a painter by profession she has also run her own antique shops and worked as an interior designer; more recently, she has begun collecting antique fabrics, pieces of lace, linen cloth, and makes cushions from these fabrics, stuffing them with a traditional filling of straw, as well as pure wool, shorn from her sheep. The house exudes this creative, eccentric style, by successfully combining French antiques with American influences, and Barbara's own quirky approach.

opposite:
The original 1940's kitchen has been spruced up with a coat of chrome paint, giving it a modern retro look. The walls are lined with hand-dyed linen.

right:
The bathroom walls are covered in a collage design, made from geometric pieces of mirror, and slivers of hand-blown glass. These add a certain artistic charm to this functional space.

railway retreat

The romance of great train adventures lives on in this converted railway carriage-cum-summerhouse in Aberdeenshire, Scotland.

Until recently the farmland of Aberdeenshire was dotted with curious farm buildings—abandoned railway carriages from the early nineteenth century. In the 1950's, a locomotive building works at Inverurie decided to sell off their old stock for the princely sum of one shilling per foot to local farmers, to use as hen houses, and storage barns. Uncared for and neglected, few of these beautiful relics have survived.

One such carriage on Mike Taitt's farm has faired slightly better. It is positioned in the open fields to enjoy prime views out across Bennachie (a mountain in the distance). The structure is only half of what was once a third class Great North Eastern Railway carriage, built in 1908. The end where the carriage was divided had been sealed with wooden boards; Mike removed these and added an extra section to this end, rather like a porch, and an additional section along one side of its length to create more space inside. Despite being run down, amazingly the Mahogany outer shell and Teak internal framework were still intact, as was the

below right:
The main section of the carriage has been transformed into a cozy sitting room. Authentic touches such as the gas lighting, luggage rack, and the wooden door with sliding window, lend an historical charm to the interior.

below:
One of two original brass regulators, this once used to control the heating in the carriage. They now control the flow of air to feed the wood-burning stove.

panelled curved pine ceiling—even most of the doors were still in place. It has been lovingly restored, with salvaged original materials: the painted tongue and groove cladding on the interior walls, the fine Mahogany door with a window that still slides up and down, and even an emergency stop handle set above one wall with a notice below warning of a fine for improper use. Many of these were rescued from other abandoned trains.

Currently the main space of the carriage provides a cozy sitting and reading area, set with a deep blue carpet and tartan covered armchair. A further section of the carriage is still to be renovated, with plans to install a sleeping area for guests, and a dining room. There is no electricity here, but a gas light lends atmospheric illumination at night, and a wood burning stove fills the interior with warmth. Indeed, Mike says that when the cold Scottish days of winter set in, he often escapes to the summerhouse because he finds it warmer here.

above:
The railway carriage is set along a deck looking out over a small pond, which the owner created for swimming in during summer. The base of the carriage is made of Teak, the upper framework is Oak, and the open door is polished Mahogany.

stone circle

Rising from the open landscape on the edge of a lake near the village of Bromham, in Wiltshire, this organic, primitive structure is eye-catching and evocative of ancient settlements. The stone and wicker circle of furniture maker Mark Wilkinson exudes a powerful connection to nature; indeed, his visitors rely upon an open fire for heat, and hope for mild, dry weather since the structure is open to the elements.

The spectacle is wholly appropriate, as this is Stonehenge country, home of the incredible and mystical stone circle which dominates Salisbury Plain, where Druids and those who follow the tradition of Wicca still gather to this day. Indeed, Mark says it was impossible not to be influenced by these elements when considering the design of the stone construction, as they create a very tangible connection to human history and ancient ancestors.

opposite:
The circle comprises chunks of local sandstone which are linked together with woven wicker panels to create a completely enclosed structure.

right:
The organic features woven within the circle's main walls echo the enchanting shapes, textures and simplicity of nature itself.

beyond the fields

A small entrance tunnel of wicker curves around the outside leading into the large inner space which is completely hidden from view from the exterior. Tall curved wicker doors open out onto the lakeside allowing stunning views of the water while still retaining the sense of enclosure. The interior is set with wooden seats around its perimeter, each of which has been built into the structure; underfoot a wooden floor has been installed to provide a smooth and levelled base.

At the center, a huge brazier provides warmth and a place to cook food: it is made from an unusual array of reclaimed parts, including an old boiler valve and a steel plate, left out in the weather to rust and age. Overhead the space is open to the sky, and by day it affords great sights of surrounding countryside, by night a covering of stars decorates the view. When seen from a distance, this seemingly incongruous mass of boulders only reveals itself as habitable from the evidence of a coil of woodsmoke that gentle emits from its heart.

Once inside, the atmosphere of the place is completely intoxicating: the simplicity of the structure, the rich colors, and patterns of the natural materials, and the wide open space conjure a sense of timelessness and presence of nature. Enclosed and protected, at least from the wind, there is also a sense of safety and seclusion in being cut off from everything else around you. Here the modern world is absolutely banished, and in its place, a retreat that can be anything your imagination might wish it to be.

With stillness surrounding the wicker walls, broken only by the occasional crackle from the fire, and lengthening shadows upon the wooden slatted floor, little surpasses this magical and remote idyll.

below:

The wicker structure is the work of a craftsperson, and provides both the practical protection from, and aesthetic alliance with, nature.

locations directory

by the sea

East Brother Light Station
San Francisco Bay, USA.
For details of bed and breakfast
accommodation, contact Gary
Herdlicka or Ann Selover.
Tel: +1 510 812 1207
website: www.ebls.org

Sea Ranch House
Pacific Coast, California, USA.
Privately owned by Ed and
Kathleen Anderson. Designed by
Turnbull, Griffin & Haesloop
Architects, 817 Bancroft Way,
Berkeley, CA 94710.
Tel: +1 510 841 9000
website: www.tgharchs.com

Mediterranean Summerhouse
Serifos island, Cyclades, Greece.
Privately owned by Suzanne Slesin
and Michael Steinberg.

Woodside Lodge
Loch Goil, West coast of Scotland.
Privately owned by Iain and Kate
Hopkins.

Hermione's House
West Sussex, England. Owned by
Alison and Marcus Riches. For
rental details, see website:
www.alimar.net

in the woods

Vermont Cabin
Vermont, USA. Owned and designed
by architect, Ross Anderson,
Anderson Architects p.c.,

55 West 25th Street, New York,
NY 10001.
Tel: +1 212 620 0996

Guesthouse Hideaway
Surrey, England. Privately owned
by landscape designer Anthony
Paul. The Hannah Peschar
Sculpture Garden, Standon Lane,
Ockley, Surrey, RH5 5QR (off A29
near Dorking) is open from the
first weekend in May to end of
October, Friday and Saturday
11am-6pm, Sundays and Bank
Holidays, 2pm-5pm.
For further information call
Tel: +44 (0)1306 627 269

Tepee
New York State, USA. Privately
owned.

The Doll House
New England, USA. Privately
owned by Gayle and John Miller.

French Hut
Cevannes, southern France.
Privately owned.

Tigh Romach
Inverness-shire, Scotland. Owned
by Joe and Leonie Gibbs.
For rental details, contact Joe,
Tel: +44 (0)1463 741336
email:Joe@belladrum.co.uk
website: www.belladrum.co.uk

in the clouds

The Mulholland Treehouse
Bodega Bay, California, USA.
Privately owned by the Holland
family.

Culloden Tower
North Yorkshire, England. Owned
by the Landmark Trust.
For rental details, or to order a
copy of The Landmark Handbook
(cost of which is refunded on first
booking), call The Landmark Trust
booking line:
Tel: +44 (0)1628 825925
website: www.Landmarktrust.co.uk

Napa Valley Hideaway
Napa Valley, California, USA.
Privately owned. Designed by
architect Ross Anderson, Anderson
Architects p.c., 55 West 25th
Street, New York, NY 10001.
Tel: +1 212 620 0996

Swiss Alpine Chalet
Ammern, Blitzingen, Switzerland.
Owned by the Wirthner family.
For rental details, contact Karoline
Wirthner at Ammern, CH-3981
Blitzingen/V5.
Tel: +41 (0)27/971 12 50

Treetop Office
Sussex, England. Privately owned.
Treehouse designed and built by
John Harris, of PearTree
(TreeHouse) Ltd.
Tel: +44 (0)1560 600111
website: www.peartreehouse.com

on the water

Silver Tassie
River Thames, Berkshire, England.
Privately owned by Gordon and
Jane Edington.

Hopbine Cottage
East Sussex, England. Privately
owned by Tony Dobinson.

Gothic Arbor
The Menagerie, Horton,
Northamptonshire, England.
Privately owned.
The Menagerie gardens are open
from April to end of September,
Mon & Thurs, 2pm-5pm and the
last Sunday of each month, 2pm-
6pm. For details call
Tel: +44 (0)1604 870957

Riverside Studio
Surrey, England. Privately owned
by landscape designer Anthony
Paul. For details of the Hannah
Peschar Sculpture Garden, see
Guesthouse Hideaway above.

in the garden

Log Cabin Summerhouse
Kent, England. Privately owned.
Cabin by rustic cabin and furniture
maker, Dave Fritchely, 2 Eggshole
Cottage, Starvecrow Lane,
Peasmarsh, East Sussex.
Tel: +44 (0)1797 230357

The Glasshouse
Schleswig-Holstein, Germany.
Privately owned and converted by
architect and interior designer
Mathias Schründer, Klosterallee
78, 20144 Hamburg.
Tel: +49 40 420 50 68

Shell Grotto
Northamptonshire, England.
Privately owned.

Pond House Garden
Isle of Wight, England. Privately
owned by Jenny Jones. Designed by
Highwater Design.
Tel: +44 (0)1983 721752
email: all@highwaterjones.com

Home Land
Devon, England. Privately owned
by artist Gary Fabian Miller.
For details of Gary's work,
contact Purdy Hicks Gallery,
65 Hopton Street, Bankside,
London, SE1 9GZ.
Tel: +44 (0)20 7401 9229

beyond the fields

The Yurt
Cornwall, England. Privately
owned by Tim Hutton.
For details of Yurts to buy or rent
and weekend yurt-making
workshops, contact Tim Hutton at
Coppice Works, Greyhayes,
St. Breward, Bodmin, Cornwall,
PL30 4LP.
Tel: +44 (0)1208 850670
website: www.copiceworks.co.uk

Highland Cottage
Inverness-shire, Scotland. Owned
by Colin and Isabella Cawdor.
For rental details of Cawdor
Cottages, contact Cawdor Estate
Office, Cawdor, Nairn, IV12 5RE.
Tel: +44 (0)1667 402402
website: www.cawdor.com

Romany Retreat
Suffolk, England. Privately owned
by traditional hurdle and rustic
furniture-maker Joe Berens.
For furniture commissions (see
summerhouse on page 7 and bench
on page 145), contact Joe,
Tel: +44 (0)1787 372871

Clapboard Farmhouse
New York State, USA. Privately
owned by Barbara Davis.
For enquiries about design
commissions, contact Barbara,
Tel: +1 607 264 3673

Railway Retreat
Aberdeen, Scotland. Privately
owned by Mike Taitt.

Stone Circle
Wiltshire, England. Privately
owned by furniture designer
Mark Wilkinson.

acknowledgments

I would like to thank all the owners of the locations featured in this book
who have allowed us to share in their delightful and inspiring places of retreat.
A special thanks to Paige Peterson for her assistance and support,
and Katherine Johnson at the Landmark Trust.